The Little Christmas

Ideas for cooking, activities, gifts, games, cards and calendars for the foundation stage at Christmas.

Written by Sally Featherstone

Illustrations by Liz Persse

The Little Book of Christmas
ISBN 1-902233-64-6

©Featherstone Education Ltd, 2001
Text ©Sally Featherstone, 2001
'Little Books' is a trade mark of Featherstone Education Ltd

First published October 2001
Reprinted January 2002

All rights reserved. No part of this publication may be reproduced, by any means, stored in a retrieval system, or transmitted in any form or by any means, electronic, mechanical, photocopying, recording or otherwise, without the prior consent of the copyright holder.

Published in the United Kingdom by
Featherstone Education Ltd
44 - 46 High Street
Husbands Bosworth
Leicestershire   LE17 6LP
tel: +44 (0)185 888 1212   fax: +44 (0)185 888 1360

Christmas in the Early Years

Christmas is one of the major festivals in the UK, and has always provided practitioners with a huge range of opportunities for planning exciting, enjoyable learning opportunities. The new Foundation curriculum allows us to ensure that during the Christmas period, activities are selected which can lead children's learning towards appropriate goals. Here are some examples of relevant goals addressed by the activities in this book:

Links with the Early Learning Goals for the Foundation Stage

PERSONAL, SOCIAL & EMOTIONAL DEVELOPMENT
- continue to be interested, excited & motivated to learn;
- have a developing respect for their own cultures & beliefs & those of other people;
- work as part of a group or class;
- understand that people have different needs, views, cultures & beliefs, which need to be treated with respect;
- understand that they can expect others to treat their needs, views, cultures & beliefs with respect.

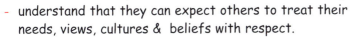

LANGUAGE, COMMUNICATION AND LITERACY
- interact with others, negotiating plans & activities & taking turns in conversations;
- enjoy listening to and using spoken and written language, and readily turn to it in their play and learning;
- listen with enjoyment and respond to stories, songs, and other music, rhymes and poems;
- extend their vocabulary, exploring the meanings & sounds of words;
- use language to imagine & recreate roles & experiences;
- use talk to organise, sequence & clarify thinking, ideas & events;
- use their phonic knowledge to write simple regular words & make phonetically plausible attempts at more complex words;
- use their phonic knowledge to write simple regular words & make phonetically plausible attempts at more complex words;
- attempt writing for various purposes, using features of different forms such as lists, stories, instructions;
- write their own names and labels.

MATHEMATICS

- say and use number names in order in familiar contexts;
- count reliably up to 10 everyday objects;
- recognise numerals 1-9;
- talk about, recognise and recreate simple patterns;
- use language such as circle, or bigger to describe the shape and size of solids and flat shapes.

KNOWLEDGE & UNDERSTANDING OF THE WORLD

- investigate objects & materials by using all of their senses;
- find out about, & identify some features of living things, objects and events they observe;
- build & construct with a wide range of objects, selecting appropriate resources, & adapting their work where necessary;
- select tools & techniques they need to shape, assemble & join the materials they are using;
- find out about & identify the uses of technology in their everyday lives & use computers to support their learning;
- begin to know about their own cultures & beliefs & those of other people.

PHYSICAL DEVELOPMENT

- use a range of small and large equipment;
- handle tools, objects, construction & malleable materials safely & with increasing control.

CREATIVE DEVELOPMENT

- explore colour, texture, shape, form & space in two & three dimensions;
- use their imagination in art & design, music, dance, imaginative & role play & stories;
- respond in a variety of ways to what they see, hear, smell, touch & feel;
- express & communicate their ideas, thoughts and feelings by using a widening range of materials, suitable tools, imaginative and role play, movement, designing and making.

Each activity in this book meets a range of these goals for learning.

Encouraging Independence

The activities in 'The Little Book of Christmas' are all intended for children to complete with the minimum of assistance from adults. Of course, you will want to offer more support to the youngest children, or those with special needs, but we would encourage you to let them do everything they can themselves.

Even the youngest children can:

☺ prepare and organise their own work area

☺ mix, measure, crack eggs, scoop mixture, ice and decorate

☺ select and cut paper, mix paint & glue, colour pasta, make cards, mount pictures, sort and organise decorations and materials

☺ choose the materials and equipment for their own work

☺ decide on the colours and way they will make pictures and patterns

☺ choose who to work with

☺ use drawing programmes

☺ write their own messages, cards and letters in 'have a go' writing, make labels, name and label their own work

☺ cut and tie string, hang and display their work, wrap presents

☺ help to clear up and put away equipment

While you concentrate on:

❋ encouraging them and asking helpful questions

❋ using opportunities to introduce new words and ideas

❋ listening to what they say

❋ observing how they work

❋ demonstrating tricky bits and finished processes

❋ handling the hot or complicated bits!

Contents

Focus of the page	page number
Introduction, early learning goals	3 and 4
Encouraging Independence	5
Cooking	
Penny Snickerdoodles	8 and 9
Mudballs	10 and 11
Gingernuts	12 and 13
Cookie Pops	14 and 15
Sticky Thumbs	16 and 17
Dancing Dough People	18 and 19
Decorations	
Dough Decorations	20 and 21
Photo Ornaments	22 and 23
Transparent Danglers	24 and 25
Apple Spice Decorations	26 and 27
Magic Painting Baubles	28 and 29
Cards	
Bauble Brooch Card	30 and 31
Stained Glass Window Cards	32 and 33
Cotton Bud Cards	34 and 35
Sleepy Sheep Cards	36 and 37
Calendars	
Sand Picture Calendars	38 and 39
With our Love - Group Calendar	40 and 41
Starry Starry Night	42 and 43
Puffy Paint	44 and 45
Roll a Rag Wrapping Paper	46 and 47
Gifts	
Glitter Pots	48 and 49
Stand up Baby Snowmen	50 and 51
Snow Storms	52 and 53
Flying Santas	54 and 55
Role play situations	
Role play - a Letter to Father Christmas	56 and 57
Role play - Story Time	58 and 59
Outside	
Frozen Decorations	60 and 61
Bird Cake	62 and 63
More Christmas Activities	64 and 65
Templates	66

Penny Snickerdoodles

Description

Make these simple sugar cookies from America, flavoured with cinnamon and shaped like pennies.

What you need for 10 to 12 dozen cookies:

150g (1 1/3 cups) of plain flour
1 teaspoon of cream of tartar
1 teaspoon of baking powder
1/2 pinch of salt
120g (1/2 cup) unsalted butter or margarine, at room temperature
150g (3/4 cup), plus 2 tablespoons sugar
1 large egg
2 teaspoons cinnamon

measuring cup or scales
a medium sized bowl
a large bowl
wooden spoon
a cup
a plate
a tablespoon
a sieve
flat baking sheets
cooling rack
knife or fish slice to lift cookies onto rack to cool
aprons
table cover

Tips for success

Wash all hands before you start, and put on aprons. Let the children do as much as they can. They can weigh and measure, mix and stir, spoon and shape, if you are there to help. Talk and listen all the time to extend vocabulary.

What you do

1. Pre-heat the oven to 200° C (400° F), Gas mark 6.
2. Into the medium bowl sift:
   the flour, cream of tartar, baking powder and salt.
3. In the large bowl, cream the butter and 150g (3/4 cup) of sugar.
4. Break the egg into a cup and then add it to the bowl.
5. Mix the egg in well.
6. Stir in the flour mixture a bit at a time, mixing well. Make sure it is thoroughly mixed in.
7. Pinch off marble sized pieces of the dough and roll into balls.
8. On a plate, mix the cinnamon and 2 tablespoons of sugar.
9. Roll the balls in the sugar and put them on the baking sheet 2 inches apart.
10. Flatten each ball slightly.
11. Bake for 6 to 10 minutes, or until the edges are light brown.
12. Transfer the cookies to the cooling rack.
13. When thoroughly cool, eat with milk or juice.

...and another thing

Make some Snickerdoodles into a gift for parents or volunteer helpers by wrapping some in cellophane and tying with a festive ribbon. Children love giving something they have made themselves.

Early learning goals

PSED - work as part of a group or class
CLL - interact with others, negotiating plans & activities & taking turns in conversations;
Ma - say and use number names in familiar contexts;
K&U - investigate objects & materials using all their senses
Phys - use a range of small and large equipment;
 - handle tools, objects, & malleable materials safely & with increasing control.
Cr - use a widening range of materials, suitable tools, designing & making

Mudballs

Description

These chocolate cookies are covered with 'snow' sugar. Even the youngest children can have fun making them with the minimum of help.

What you need for 4 dozen mudballs:

250g (1 cup) butter/margarine
55g (2 oz) chocolate (melted)
150g (2/3 cup) of sugar
1 egg yolk
1½ teaspoons of vanilla essence
280g (2 cups) of flour
¼ teaspoon of salt
100g (¾ cup) of chopped walnuts or almonds
<u>and for the 'snow'</u>
200g (¾ cup) of icing sugar
3 tablespoons cocoa powder

measuring cup or scales
a large bowl
a wooden spoon
a small bowl and a pan or bowl of very hot water (adult)
a tablespoon
cling film
flat baking sheets
knife or fish slice to lift cookies onto rack to cool
cooling rack
a plate to mix the snow
a sieve
aprons, table cover

Tips for success

Melting chocolate can be done in a microwave or over a pan of hot water. Very young children should not be directly involved in this part of the recipe, but they can watch an adult if carefully supervised, and they enjoy seeing how the chocolate changes.

What you do

1. Help them to cream the butter/margarine in the bowl.
2. Melt the chocolate in a small bowl over hot water (adult only).
3. Add the melted chocolate to the butter/margarine and blend well.
4. Add the sugar, egg yolk and vanilla essence, stirring well.
5. Add the flour and salt a bit at a time. stirring until the mixture is smooth.
6. Add the nuts and stir again.
7. Put the dough in the fridge (or a cold place) for 1hr.
8. Heat the oven to 180C (350°F) Gas mark 4.
9. Scoop out small tablespoons full of the mixture and roll into balls between hands. (Let them do it!). Put on ungreased baking sheets, leaving 1" between.
10. Bake for 10-12 minutes until the tops of the cookies set.
11. Mix the icing sugar and cocoa powder on a plate.
12. Cool the mudballs for 5 minutes, toss them in the snow, and put them on a cooling rack. (adult help)
13. Cool completely, then dust again with snow.
14. Store in an airtight container (if you don't eat them all!)

...and another thing

You could make these mudballs into a lovely gift by putting a few in the middle of a square of cellophane or tissue and tying them up with a ribbon or some Christmas string.

Early learning goals

PSED - work as part of a group or class
CLL - interact with others, negotiating plans & activities & taking turns in conversations;
Ma - say and use number names in familiar contexts;
K&U - investigate objects & materials using all their senses
Phys - use a range of small and large equipment;
 - handle tools, objects, & malleable materials safely & with increasing control.
Cr - use a widening range of materials, suitable tools, designing & making

Ginger Nuts

Description

A classic recipe for crispy biscuits, which are easy to bake and make an inexpensive and welcome gift.

What you need for 10 dozen ginger nuts:

325g (2¼ cups) flour
2 teaspoons of baking powder
1 teaspoon of cinnamon
1 teaspoon of powdered ginger
¼ teaspoon of nutmeg
¼ teaspoon of ground cloves
¼ teaspoon of salt
¼ teaspoon of salt
175g (¾ cup) butter/margarine
175g (1 cup) soft brown sugar
60ml (¼ cup) of black treacle or molasses
1 large egg

sugar for coating
measuring cup or scales
2 large bowls
a wooden spoon
a tablespoon
a teaspoon
a very tiny teaspoon
flat baking sheets
knife or fish slice to lift cookies onto rack to cool
cooling rack
a plate for sugar coating
a sieve
aprons, table cover

Tips for success

If you make these ginger nuts really tiny, you will be surprised how many you can get out of one batch. Try using a coffee spoon, or even a spoon from a dolls' teaset. Remember, tiny biscuits take a shorter time to cook, and you may need to adjust the cooking time for your oven.

What you do

1. Try smelling all the different spices before you start.
2. Help them to mix together the flour, baking powder, spices and salt in one bowl.
3. In the other bowl cream the butter and sugar.
4. Add the egg and the molasses or black treacle to the butter and sugar, stirring well.
5. Add the flour and spice mixture a bit at a time. stirring until the mixture is smooth.
6. Cover and put in the fridge (or a cold place) for an hour.
7. Heat the oven to 190°C (375°F) Gas mark 5.
8. Use a tiny teaspoon to scoop out the dough and roll into balls between hands. (Let them do it!)
9. Put some granulated sugar on a plate and roll each ball in sugar and put them on an ungreased baking sheet.
10. Bake for 7-9 minutes until they are crunchy and set.
11. Use a knife or slice to lift them onto a cooling tray <u>while they are still hot</u>.
12. Cool completely before eating.
13. Store in an airtight container for up to a week or a freezer for a month(if you don't eat them all!).

...and another thing

Try making some gingerbread baskets. Scoop more mixture to make bigger biscuits, and <u>when cooked, but still hot</u>, lift them carefully onto a clean orange or tangerine. The hot biscuit will cover the top of the orange, and you can lift it off when it cools and hardens. Turn it over and you have a basket to fill with sweets or nuts.

Early learning goals

<u>PSED</u> - work as part of a group or class
<u>CLL</u> - interact with others, negotiating plans & activities & taking turns in conversations;
<u>Ma</u> - say and use number names in familiar contexts;
<u>K&U</u>- investigate objects & materials using all their senses
<u>Phys</u> - use a range of small and large equipment;
- handle tools, objects, & malleable materials safely & with increasing control.
<u>Cr</u> - use a widening range of materials, suitable tools, designing & making

Cookie Pops

Description

Here is a different way to make lollipops - it uses a simple biscuit dough, with chocolate surprises.

What you need for 24 lollies:

1 egg
100g (½ cup) granulated sugar
100g (½ cup) soft brown sugar
100g (½ cup) soft margarine
220g (1½ cups of flour
½ teaspoon of baking powder
½ teaspoon of salt
1 cup of candy coated chocolate sweets (M&M's or Smarties)
wooden lolly sticks

measuring cup or scales
a large bowl
a wooden spoon
a teaspoon
flat baking sheets
knife or fish slice to lift cookies onto rack to cool
cooling rack
aprons, table cover

Tips for success

Make sure the sticks are pushed in at least half way through the dough, or they may fall off in the middle of eating!

This is another recipe that even the youngest children can make on their own (except for the baking!).

What you do

1. Heat the oven to 190°C (375°F) Gas mark 5.
2. Crack the egg into the bowl, letting the egg slide down the side of the bowl.
3. Add the granulated and the brown sugar. Stir well.
4. Add the flour, baking powder and salt. Mix well.
5. Stir the sweets into the dough.
6. Scoop out tablespoonfuls of mixture onto the baking sheet.
7. Push a lolly stick into each cookie.
8. Bake for 10 to 12 minutes until the cookie-pops are light brown.
8. Remove from the oven and leave to cool for 2 minutes.
9. Lift carefully with the slice onto the wire rack.
10. Leave to finish cooling before eating!

P.S. You can make chocolate chip lollies the same way - use 1 cup of chocolate chips instead of the sweets.

...and another thing

You can also make cookie lollies with the sort of dough that needs rolling. Just roll out the mixture, cut two of each shape and sandwich a lolly stick between the two shapes. Bake as suggested in the recipe, but remember, thicker things take longer to cook.

Early learning goals
- PSED - work as part of a group or class
- CLL - interact with others, negotiating plans & activities & taking turns in conversations;
- Ma - say and use number names in familiar contexts;
- K&U - investigate objects & materials using all their senses
- Phys - use a range of small and large equipment;
- - handle tools, objects, & malleable materials safely & with increasing control.
- Cr - use a widening range of materials, suitable tools, designing & making

Sticky Thumbs

Description

A very simple recipe for younger children, which older ones will still enjoy.

What you need for 4 dozen biscuits:

225g (1 cup) butter/margarine
75g (½ cup) of brown sugar
1 large egg
1 teaspoon of vanilla essence
425g (3 cups) of flour
½ teaspoon of salt

granulated sugar for rolling
jam or jelly for filling

measuring cup or scales
a large bowl
a wooden spoon
a tablespoon
a teaspoon
flat baking sheets
knife or fish slice to lift cookies onto rack to cool
cooling rack
a plate for the dipping sugar
aprons, table cover

Tips for success

Work with a small number of children at a time, and while they work, discuss the feel and texture of the ingredients - the sugar, the dough, the egg. Talk about the smell of the vanilla, the brown sugar, the jam.

The children can do all the steps in this recipe, apart from the hot bits! Let them measure, weigh, mix and crack eggs. Talk about the changes to the ingredients at each stage.

What you do

1. Mix the butter and sugar together until creamy.
2. Break the egg into the mixture, and mix well.
3. Add the flour and the salt.
4. Put in the fridge or a cold place until stiff enough to roll into balls.
5. Heat the oven to 160°C (325°F) gas mark 3.
6. Scoop out spoonfuls of dough and make into one inch (2.5 cm.) balls.
7. Put some sugar on a plate and roll each ball in sugar
8. Put the balls on a baking sheet and push a thumb into each ball, making a good hollow.
   If the dough cracks, just push it together again.
9. Fill each hole with half a teaspoon of jam or jelly.
10. Bake for 10-12 minutes.
11. Lift onto a wire rack to cool.

Remember - Jam stays hot for a long time. Check to make sure they are really cool before eating.

...and another thing

Try baking the Sticky Thumbs empty, then put a sweet, some chocolate chips or a raspberry inside each, while they are still warm.

Early learning goals
PSED - work as part of a group or class
CLL - interact with others, negotiating plans & activities & taking turns in conversations;
Ma - say and use number names in familiar contexts;
K&U - investigate objects & materials using all their senses
Phys - use a range of small and large equipment;
 - handle tools, objects, & malleable materials safely & with increasing control.
Cr - use a widening range of materials, suitable tools, designing & making

Dancing Dough People

Description

Individual spicy biscuit figures to hang in a window or on a tree. They also make great edible gift tags!

What you need for 24 dough people:

550g (4½ cups) plain flour
1 teaspoon of baking powder
1 tablespoon ground cinnamon
1 teaspoon ground ginger
100g (½ cup) butter/margarine, plus a bit for greasing trays
125g (¾ cup) soft brown sugar
2 eggs
125g (¾ cup) molasses or black treacle
white & coloured icing or icing pens
sprinkles, silver balls, jellies
measuring cup or scales
2 large bowls
a wooden spoon
a rolling pin
a tablespoon
a teaspoon
gingerbread cutters
a straw for making holes
flat baking sheets
knife or spatula to lift figures onto rack to cool
cooling rack
plates or cups to hold decorations
aprons, table cover
decorative string for hanging

Tips for success

If you haven't got a gingerbread cutter, draw a shape on thick card and cut it out to make your own.
Put the decorations in paper cake cases or a bun tin, so each child has their own for decorating. Use liquorice strings to make smiles and stripey jumpers.

What you do

1. Try smelling the spices before you start!
2. Mix the flour, baking powder, spices and salt in a bowl.
3. In the other bowl cream the butter and sugar.
4. Add the eggs one at a time
5. Add the molasses or black treacle to this mixture, stirring well.
5. Add the flour and spice mixture a bit at a time. stirring until the mixture is well mixed.
6. Cover and put in the fridge (or a cold place) for an hour.
7. Heat the oven to 180C (350°F) Gas mark 4, and grease some trays with margarine or oil.
8. Sprinkle flour on a clean surface and roll out half the dough to about half an inch thick.
9. Cut out people shapes and transfer them to the baking trays. Make a hole with the straw for hanging.
10. Now get the children to gently move the arms and legs to make each figure 'dance'.
11. Bake for 10-12 minutes until they are crunchy and set.
12. Use a knife or slice to lift them onto a cooling tray.
13. Cool completely before decorating with icing etc.

...and another thing

You can also use this recipe for tree shapes, houses or even a whole gingerbread house. Cut four rectangles for the walls, two rectangles for the roof and stick them together with icing. Put on an iced board, decorate with small sweets and cake decorations and add 'small world' trees and people for a snow scene.

Early learning goals

PSED - have a developing respect for their own cultures & beliefs
CLL - interact with others, negotiating plans & activities
 - write their own names & labels
Ma - count reliably up to 10
 - use language to describe shape
K&U - investigate objects & materials by using all of their senses
 - select tools & techniques they need to shape materials
Phys - use a range of equipment;
 - handle tools, object
Cr - explore colour, texture, shape, form & space
 - respond to what they see, hear, smell, touch & feel

Dough Decorations

Description

These decorations are <u>not</u> for eating! Hang them on a tree or in a window. They also make great gifts.

What you need for 25 small ornaments:

For the dough:
- 550g (4 cups) of plain flour
- 1 cup of salt
- 375ml (1½ cups) of water
- red or green paint or food colouring (if you like)

to decorate:
- sequins
- glitter
- paint with added glue
- string to hang them up

- measuring cup or scales
- a large bowl
- a wooden spoon
- boards or a clean table
- rolling pins
- small cutters (seasonal shapes, stars, trees, circles etc) or playdough stamps
- straws to make holes for string
- flat baking sheets
- knife or fish slice to lift cookies onto rack to cool
- cooling rack
- aprons, table cover

Tips for success

For very young children, make balls of dough and use dough stamps (you can get these on bought packs of playdough). For all dough decorations, a top coat of white glue diluted with twice as much water will seal the decorations and make them shine.

Children can do all the steps of this recipe apart from the hot bits, but they need reminding that this is <u>not</u> an eating recipe.

What you do

1. Mix the flour, salt and water.
2. Add colouring if you want.
3. Knead it well until it is smooth.
4. Take some dough and roll or flatten it on a board. Use cutters or dough stamps to make shapes.
5. Make a hole in each with a straw.
6. Put the decorations on a baking sheet and bake for 1 to 1.5 hours at 160°C (325°F) gas mark 3.
   If you put a named piece of paper under each child's decorations on the baking tray it will be easier to remember whose is which. When they are baked, you (or they) can write initials or names on the backs with a marker pen.
7. Dry for a day or two (if they can wait!) to make sure all the water has evaporated.
8. Decorate with sequins, glitter and paint.
9. Leave to dry then coat with PVA 'varnish'.
10. Hang a gold or red string through each.

...and another thing

Why not use this recipe to make a nativity scene or other Christmas story? tell the story, then make flat dough characters and stick them on a big painted sheet of card or hang them against a window painted with a suitable scene.

Early learning goals
<u>PSED</u> - have a developing respect for their own cultures & beliefs
<u>CLL</u> - interact with others, negotiating plans & activities
 - write their own names & labels
<u>Ma</u> - count reliably up to 10
 - use language to describe shape
<u>K&U</u> - investigate objects & materials by using all of their senses
 - select tools & techniques they need to shape materials
<u>Phys</u> - use a range of equipment;
 - handle tools, object
<u>Cr</u> - explore colour, texture, shape, form & space
 - respond to what they see, hear, smell, touch & feel;

Photo Ornaments

Description

If you have a digital camera, make some unique ornaments for families to treasure.

What you need for photo ornaments:

small photos of each child (print on paper, not card)
<u>plastic</u> tree baubles
small sticks (e.g. lolly sticks)
small squares of thick card (foil covered if possible)
white glue, slightly diluted with water
scissors
zig-zag/pattern cut scissors

coloured string or thin ribbon for hanging
sequins
glitter
thin tinsel
coloured or wrapping paper
permanent markers (black, gold, silver)

Tips for success

If you are working on baubles or a curved surface, use smaller photos, so they stick easily.
If you decide to make frames with sticks, you could collect some twigs on a walk or in the garden.

What you do

1. Put the photos and decorations in containers.
2. Show the children how to either:
   - choose a photo to stick on a bauble
   - tie or glue three or four sticks together to make a frame and stick a photo behind it
   - stick their picture on a foil card shape
3. The children can then decorate their photo in any way they choose, with the things on offer.
4. Leave to dry.
5. With a permanent marker, write the date and the child's name in any space available.
6. Add a string to the decoration
7. Hang the decorations up until it is time to take them home (or keep them secret for a really great surprise gift on the last day of school).

P.S. You could make digital photos into great cards or calendars (how about a group or class photo on a card for each family?). This would be a good alternative to the holly and robins!

...and another thing

You could use digital photos to make an advent calendar. sticking a different child's photo on each door and opening one each day.

Early learning goals
PSED - treat needs, views, cultures & beliefs with respect.
CLL - write own names & labels
Ma - use language such as circle, or bigger to describe shape & size
K&U - investigate objects & materials by using all of their senses
 - use computers to support their learning;
Phys - use a range of equipment
 - handle tools & objects safely & with increasing control.
Cr - explore colour, texture, shape, form & space in 2 & 3 dimensions

Transparent Dangles

Description

This is a simple and effective way to make hanging decorations. Any child can make them and they look stunning.

What you need for transparent dangles:

- white or pastel coloured tissue paper
- small bits of shiny paper and fabric
- sequins, stars
- beads
- glitter
- silver and gold string
- small seeds (e.g. budgie seed)
- small pasta shapes (stars, letters etc)
- white glue diluted with water
- glue or paste brushes (better than spreaders for this job)
- plastic sheeting or dustbin liners
- masking tape
- scissors
- aprons

Tips for success

Don't be put off by the look of these ornaments when they are wet! Remember that white glue dries clear and when they are finished they will be great! Spend time with the children while they are working, but try not to interfere with their sense of pattern and order.

What you do

1. Stick some plastic or an opened-up bin liner on the table with masking tape. Several children can work at the table at one time.
2. Put the sequins etc in saucers or plastic food trays.
3. Tear some squares and circles from tissue paper (about 12" or 30cm across).
4. Show the children how to spread glue on the plastic and stick a piece of tissue down.
5. Spread more glue on the top of the tissue and start to make a design with the collage bits.
6. When they are happy with their design, cover it with another sheet of tissue and paste again with glue.
7. Leave to dry (preferably over night).
8. Carefully separate the design from the plastic. If it is really dry, it will come off quite easily, and the children can help. The resulting design will be an almost transparent surprise, with the design 'trapped' between two layers in a sandwich.
9. Trim any straggly bits.
10. Hang on strings against the windows or across the room.

...and another thing

These make lovely gifts as window ornaments. Or try making a really big design as a collaborative activity and use the result to cover a whole window, or make a screen or divider in the room by mounting it in a big picture frame, painted gold.

Early learning goals

PSED - continue to be interested, excited & motivated to learn
- work as part of a group or class
CLL - interact with others, negotiating plans & activities & taking turns in conversations;
K&U - construct with a wide range of objects, selecting appropriate resources
Phys - use a range of equipment;
- handle tools, objects, materials safely & with increasing control.
Cr - explore colour, texture, shape, form & space
- respond in a variety of ways to what they see, smell, touch & feel

Apple Spice Smells Nice

Description

Use this unusual dough to make perfumed decorations. But make sure the children know they are definitely <u>not</u> for eating!!

What you need for spice decorations

25ml (1 cup) apple sauce (the smooth, canned or bottled type)
225g (1½ cups of ground cinnamon)
white glue to mix

measuring cup or jug
a bowl (not used afterwards for food)
cling film or plastic bag
rolling pins
small festive cutters
board or smooth surface
a straw to make holes for hanging
wire cooling rack
spatula or knife
ribbon or festive string
aprons, table cover

Tips for success

This recipe uses a large amount of spice. Buy ground cinnamon in large quantities from Asian grocers or supermarkets - its much cheaper. You need to add the white glue slowly and gauge the amount.

What you do

1. Mix all ingredients together into a stiff dough, adding the glue bit by bit until the dough feels stiff.
2. Form into a ball and cover with cling film (or put in a plastic bag).
3. Chill for 30 minutes (in a fridge or outside) until stiff.
4. Sprinkle more cinnamon on a board or flat surface andgive each child some dough.
5. Roll out to 1/2" (1cm) - no thinner.
6. Cut out shapes with cutters.
7. Make a hole in each with the straw.
8. Lift carefully onto the wire rack.
9. Leave to dry for about 2 days.
10. Glaze with slightly diluted white glue to make them shiny.
11. Hang on a ribbon or string

Don't forget to smell, talk about and taste the ingredients (where appropriate!) and talk about the texture and smell of the dough as they work.

...and another thing

You could get children to cut around their own hands (with help and a very blunt knife or clay tool) and mount these on board for a unique perfumed calendar or card.

Early learning goals
PSED - have a developing respect for cultures & beliefs
CLL - interact with others, negotiating plans & activities
 - write their own names & labels
Ma - count reliably up to 10
 - use language to describe shape
K&U - investigate objects & materials by using all of their senses
 - select tools & techniques they need to shape materials
Phys - use a range of equipment;
 - handle tools, object
Cr - explore colour, texture,shape, form & space
 - respond to what they see, hear, smell, touch & feel

Magic Painting Baubles

Description

Simple wax resist is used to create unbreakable baubles which will be treasured for years. The magic is revealed when the ball is dipped.

What you need for magic painting:

- a ping pong ball for each child
- white candles or white wax crayons
- food colouring
- water
- a long bodkin or thick needle
- festive string or ribbon
- sequins and glitter
- large bowls
- a spoon
- a coat hanger for drying baubles
- clothes pegs
- white glue and spreaders
- aprons, table cover, newspaper
- plastic gloves (optional)

Tips for success

Use red and green colouring for a festive look.
Make sure the children put plenty of wax on the ball to make the pattern interesting.
Talk about what happens when you dip the balls in the colouring.

What you do

1. Punch a hole in each side of the ball with the bodkin (adult activity).
2. Use the long needle to thread a string through the holes. Tie a good knot in the end.
3. Mix some bowls of food colouring and water.
4. Explain the process and talk about what they need to do.
5. Each child uses the white wax crayons or candles to scribble or draw on their ball.
6. When they have completed their invisible design, they can dip the ball in a colour of their choice - holding on to the string.
7. Count to 20 before removing the ball from the colouring.
8. Use clothes pegs to clip the baubles on the coat hanger or a line to dry. (Put newspaper under to catch drips.)
9. When dry, decorate with sequins and glitter if they like.
10. Help them write their name and the year on the bauble with a waterproof marker.
11. Hang on a tree or a string across the room until the end of term.

P.S. Make some extra ones for helpers or other friends.

....and another thing

Gold and silver pens make the baubles extra sparkly!
Wax resist can also be used for cards and calendars. Draw on white paper, brush with dilute colouring to see the image appear. Mount on card and add a message.

Early learning goals

PSED - continue to be interested, excited & motivated to learn
- work as part of a group or class
CLL - interact with others, negotiating plans & activities & taking turns in conversations;
K&U - construct with a wide range of objects, selecting appropriate resources
Phys - use a range of equipment;
- handle tools, objects, materials safely & with increasing control.
Cr - explore colour, texture, shape, form & space
- respond in a variety of ways to what they see, smell, touch & feel

Bauble Brooch Card

Description
A collaborative activity resulting in a most unusual gift.

What you need for brooch cards:
a large sheet of foil covered card (A2 or A1 size)
white glue and spreaders
sequins, glitter
puffy paint (see page 44)
brooch pins (1 for each child)
white card pieces (A5) for the greeting cards
small sheets of coloured tissue paper
thin ribbon or decorative string
squeezy bottles
containers for sequins, glitter
aprons, table cover
sharp adult scissors

Tips for success
Use slightly dilute white glue for the collage stage. If you have access to a hot glue gun, use this to stick the brooch pins (N.B. <u>children should never use hot glue guns</u>). Do the writing inside the cards before putting the brooches on the front - it's easier.

What you do

1. Tape one or several large sheets of foil card to table tops.
2. Put out sequins, glitter, glue, puffy paint, and let the children decorate the sheets in groups over a day. Encourage them to explore and have fun with the resources, working together and talking about what they do.
3. At the end of the session, paint a coat of dilute white glue over the whole collage and leave to dry.
4. When dry, with the children, turn the card over and, on the back, draw circles (round an egg cup, cookie cutter or small glass). Make enough for one each and some spares for friends, helpers etc.
5. An adult will need to cut the circles out with sharp scissors, and stick the pins on the back (but children could watch and learn!)
6. Fold the white cards in half and do the writing inside
7. Show the children how to stick a square of tissue paper on the front of the card. Then pin a brooch through each card, adding a bow of gold string or red ribbon.

...and another thing

Make a few extra brooches for all the staff who will want one! Use the snippings to make mobiles, or stick them back to back as decorations and hang them on a tree or in a window. Or make gift tags for the Christmas Fair!

Early learning goals

PSED - continue to be interested, excited & motivated to learn
- work as part of a group or class
CLL - interact with others, negotiating plans & activities & taking turns in conversations;
K&U - construct with a wide range of objects, selecting appropriate resources
Phys - use a range of equipment;
- handle tools, objects, materials safely & with increasing control.
Cr - explore colour, texture, shape, form & space
- respond in a variety of ways to what they see, smell, touch & feel

Stained Glass Windows

Description

An easy way to make an effective card or calendar. This method makes everyone's picture look glowingly great!

What you need for stained glass cards:

one paper plate for each child
pieces of smooth, thin white paper
felt pens
cooking oil
cotton wool balls
string or ribbon for hanging
calendar tabs (optional)

white glue
spreaders
scissors
a permanent marker
aprons, table cover

Tips for success

Children can do most of this on their own. They just need you for the plate cutting and the difficult sticking. You may like to let them practice the method before deciding which picture they want to make into the final hanging.

What you do

1. Cut the centre from one of the plates.
2. Using this as a guide, draw circles on the pieces of white paper (photocopy paper works well)
3. Offer the felt pens and paper to children as a drawing activity. Explain why the circles have been drawn (or let them draw their own). Sit with them to encourage concentration and discussion. You may want to suggest a theme.
4. When the drawings are done, turn the paper over and show the children how to rub a little cooking oil on the back of the picture with a cotton ball.
5. Leave to dry for at least 2 hours.
6. Cut the picture out, leaving 3cm (1") outside the circle.
7. Stick the picture to the back of the plate with white glue or tape, so the picture fits the hole.
8. Write (or let them write) their name round the edge of the plate, and decorate the edges (dilute food colouring and cotton buds is easy and effective).
9. Stick a string on the back to hang, and add a calendar tab to make it into a calendar if you wish.

...and another thing

These pictures look best with a window or a light behind them. Hang against your windows or on a mirror. This method can also be used to construct a big, collaborative window design on a large piece of paper.

early learning goals

PSED - continue to be interested, excited & motivated to learn
CLL - extend their vocabulary, exploring the meanings of words
 - use talk to organise, sequence & clarify thinking, ideas, events;
 - write their own names & labels
Ma - use language to describe shape and size
K&U - investigate objects & materials by using all of their senses
 - select tools & techniques
Phys - use a range of equipment;
 - handle tools, objects, materials
Cr - explore colour, texture, shape, form & space

Cotton Bud Cards

Description

Cotton buds give children real practice in using small tools. They will enjoy making these mini-pictures into cards to take home.

What you need for cotton bud cards:

card (A4 or A5 folded in half)
cotton buds or Q/tips
plates, saucers or plastic lids
food colouring
water in small pots or jars
(e.g. baby food jars)
squares of paper to fit fronts of cards
masking tape

scissors
aprons
table cover

Tips for success

This activity needs an adult present, to talk and encourage concentration. Encourage the children to experiment with pictures and patterns before deciding which one they will use for their card.

What you do

1. Place a few drops of colour in each saucer or lid. Add a drop or two of water (but only a drop!)
2. Put some cotton buds by each colour.
3. Tape some paper squares to the table with masking tape (it comes off easily without tearing the paper)
4. Show the children how to take a dip of colour and use the cotton bud to make marks, patterns and pictures on the paper.
5. Be available for discussion and help if necessary.
6. Leave to dry.
7. Help them select a picture and stick on the front of cards.
8. Draw a frame round the picture with a felt pen.
9. Help the children to write their names inside the card.

Try the same technique with gold and silver paint on black card for gift tags.
Try the same technique on wet paper and talk about what happens.

...and another thing

If you feel adventurous, let the children use this technique with paint on a window, clear plastic or a mirror. Combine it with sequins, cellophane paper and tissue. When you need to, remove it from the glass, use warm soapy water and a plastic scraper.

Early learning goals
PSED - continue to be interested, excited & motivated to learn
CLL - use talk to organise, sequence & clarify thinking, ideas, & events;
 - write their own names & labels
Ma - talk about, recognise and recreate simple patterns;
K&U - investigate objects & materials by using all of their senses
Phys - use a range of equipment;
 - handle tools, safely
Cr - explore colour, texture, shape, form & space in 2 dimensions
 - use their imagination in art & design

Sleepy Sheep

Description

Rocking sheep cards are easy to make and a bit different. Older children can make them almost unaided, younger children will need some help.

What you need for sleepy sheep:

white and green card
black sticky paper
white or pale yellow cotton
wool
paper fasteners
glue and spreaders
crayons
felt pens

a saucer
the templates from the back of this book
scissors
a pencil
some plasticene or Blutack
aprons, table cover

Tips for success

When children are making holes in card, show them how to put a ball of plasticene on the table and let them use a pencil to push through the card and into the plasticene. This way, they will be able to make holes safely by themselves.

What you do

1. Trace and cut out the templates (or make your own)
2. Make an example, so the children understand what they are going to do.
3. Draw round the saucer.
4. Cut the circle out and fold in half.
5. You might like to suggest they do the writing inside at this stage - it's easier. Felt pen works best on card.
6. Trace and cut out the body and head of the sheep.
7. Draw eyes and a mouth.
8. Colour the ears black.
9. Stick a blob of cotton wool between the ears for 'hair'.
10. Glue the body and cover with cotton wool.
11. Push a pencil through the head and the body at X. Use a paper fastener to fix the head and body together so the head will move.
12. Now stick the body onto the middle of the card.
13. Cut two legs from black paper and stick on below the body.
14. The Rock-a-bye sheep is finished, and will rock if pushed gently with a finger.

...and another thing

You could use this design to make rocking cards for other greetings (flowers for Mother's Day or Father's Day, candles for Diwali, hearts for a valentine, chicks for Spring etc).

Early learning goals

PSED - continue to be interested, excited & motivated to learn
CLL - extend their vocabulary, exploring the meanings of words
 - use talk to sequence events;
 - write their own names & messages
K&U - investigate objects & materials by using all of their senses
 - select tools & techniques they need to shape & join materials
Phys - use a range of equipment;
Cr - explore colour, texture, shape, form & space
 - respond in a variety of ways to what they see, hear, smell, touch & feel

Sand 'Timers'

Description

Use this simple method to make sand pictures for calendars. Children of all ages enjoy working with coloured sand and glue.

What you need for sand timers:

Stage 1
silver sand
food colouring
plastic bags (zip lock type)

Stage 2
containers (see below)
white glue and spreaders
black felt pens or chalk
a selection of pieces of strong paper about 20cm. (8") sq.
a tray or tin, to keep the sand in control!

Stage 3
card for backing
string or ribbon for hanging
calendar tabs
aprons, table cover

Tips for success

Make the coloured sand on one day and the pictures on another. The method works best if the sand is very dry. Try using flour sifters for sprinkling the sand, or pouring it from little cups or jugs. Stick to simple shapes.

What you do

1. Put a cup of dry sand in a plastic bag. Add food colouring and a few drops of water.
2. Close the bag and squeeze the bag around until all the sand is coloured evenly. Add more colour if you need to. Children love doing this, and talking about what happens.
3. Repeat steps 1 and 2 with other colours.
4. Tip the coloured sand onto trays and dry on a radiator or in a low oven until it is thoroughly dried out. (Don't put it in a microwave!)
5. Offer the children black markers or chalk to make patterns or pictures on the paper. Explain that the shapes will be filled with sand, so they need to be simple outlines.
6. Put the paper on a tray and glue one part of the picture at a time. Choose a coloured sand for each piece and sprinkle generously. Shake excess back into container.
7. Continue until the design is covered.
8. Leave to dry overnight.
9. Mount on card, punch holes for ribbon or string.
10. Add a calendar tab and perhaps a felt pen frame.

...and another thing

This method is good for collaborative work on a big picture. Try taping some card to the ground outside, drawing a pattern with felt pens and filling with coloured sand. Or you could make a more permanent picture by using plaster or a thin layer of cement on a path or paving.

Early learning goals

PSED - continue to be interested, excited & motivated to learn
 - work as part of a group or class
CLL - interact with others, negotiating plans & activities & taking turns in conversations;
K&U - selecting appropriate resources
Phys - use a range of equipment;
 - handle tools, objects, materials safely & with increasing control.
Cr - explore colour, texture, shape, form & space
 - respond in a variety of ways to what they see, smell, touch & feel

With Love From All of Us

Description

If you have a digital camera, this is a good way to use it! Parents and children love having each others pictures and feeling part of a group.

What you need for group pictures:

calendar tabs
small versions of photos of each child, or
small versions of pictures drawn by each child (if you have a drawing programme on the computer, print these very small and in multiple versions on a page)

waterproof markers
sheets of card
ribbon or festive string
white glue and spreaders
aprons, table cover

Tips for success

Explore the ways your computer will provide you with multiple copies of photos or pictures. Otherwise, use the photocopier and reduce them down. You could always take a picture of the whole class or group and use that.

What you do

1. Make multiple copies of the pictures you will offer the children.
2. Sort and organise them in little pots or divided containers such as plastic food trays.
3. Each child chooses a piece of card and selects pictures to stick in a pattern or a collage. Let them decide which children and which pictures to use. Talk about this as they work.
4. When the design is completed, leave to dry.
5. When dry, cover with a coat of slightly diluted white glue to glaze.
6. Add a calendar tab and ribbon, and help each child to write their name and the year in waterproof marker.

N.B. You may need to put the completed calendars under a heavy book or weight for a day or so to flatten them.

Hang the calendars on a board backed with child designed paper (see page 46).

...and another thing

A good fund raiser: Choose 12 pictures drawn by children in the class or group(you may want to arrange collaborative pictures so everyone is included. Add names and a month's dates to each, and make these into a month by month calendar to sell to parents.

Early learning goals
PSED - continue to be interested, excited & motivated to learn
CLL - extend their vocabulary, exploring the meanings of words
 - use talk to organise, sequence & clarify thinking, ideas, events;
 - write their own names & labels
K&U - investigate objects & materials by using all of their senses
 - select tools & techniques
Phys - use a range of equipment;
 - handle tools, objects, materials
Cr - explore colour, texture, shape, form & space
 - respond in a variety of ways to what they see, touch & feel

Starry, Starry Night

Description

You can use this technique to make calendars, cards, hangings or even to print teeshirts. The method is simple, the effect is stunning.

What you need for winter night scenes:

- pieces of white or pastel coloured fabric (sheeting, teeshirt material, old pillow cases etc)
- blue and white paint to mix for night shades
- card, string, calendar tabs etc
- small sponges
- saucers or containers for paint
- masking tape
- newspaper
- self adhesive stars, moons and other shapes
- aprons, table cover

Tips for success

New material should always be washed before using, or the paint doesn't fix properly. Using self adhesive shapes is easiest, but you could use paper shapes and stick them down with dabs of wallpaper paste.

What you do

1. Cut some pieces of fabric (small for cards, larger for calendars).
2. With the children, mix some shades of blue paint and put in shallow dishes or saucers. You could add a bit of black to make a really midnight blue. Test the colours on some scraps of fabric. Talk about what happens as they mix the paint.
3. Put out the shapes, so the children can choose.
4. Tape some pieces of fabric to a table with masking tape to avoid wrinkling. If you want to make a tidy 'frame' to the picture, put a strip of tape along each side, overlapping the edge evenly and securing it to the table.
5. Stick stars and other shapes all over the fabric (stars are the most effective). Press down well.
6. Sponge print over the whole piece, covering the stars as well. Let them choose how to use the blue shades.
7. Leave for a few minutes to begin drying.
8. Peel off the stars and other shapes to leave a night sky!
9. Mount on cards or calendars.

....and another thing

Try this method on clear plastic and hang it in front of a light. Use some bigger stars and a clear shower curtain to make a hanging (put a bit of white glue in the paint to make it stick better and shine). This method makes great pond, sea and summer backgrounds too.

Early learning goals

PSED - continue to be interested, excited & motivated to learn
CLL - extend their vocabulary, exploring the meanings of words
 - use talk to organise, sequence & clarify thinking, ideas, events;
 - write their own names & labels
Ma - use language to describe shape and size
K&U - investigate objects & materials by using all of their senses
 - select tools & techniques
Phys - use a range of equipment;
 - handle tools, objects, materials
Cr - explore colour, texture, shape, form & space

Puffy Paint

Description

Paint a card or calendar picture with this paint, which puffs up as it dries.

What you need for puffy paint:

For each colour you want to make:
- 150g (1 cup) of white flour
- 150g (1 cup) of salt
- 8fl oz (1 cup) of water
- ready mixed paint

You also need one or more empty plastic squeezy bottles from washing up liquid

- measuring cup or scales
- a bowl
- a spoon
- a funnel
- paper or card
- glitter

- aprons, table cover

Tips for success

Use this paint within two days. After that it won't work.

What you do

1. Mix the flour, salt and water. If you want several colours, increase the amounts of each ingredient.
2. Divide the liquid between the squeezy bottles. Use a funnel!
3. Add paint to each bottle, put on the top and give it a shake to mix.
4. Use the bottles to paint pictures and patterns on thin card or thick paper.
5. Watch the paint as it dries, and feel it when it is dry. The paint will puff up as it dries, leaving a raised picture or pattern
6. Mount the pictures on cards or calendars.

* sprinkle glitter on the paint while it is still wet for an extra sparkle
* try using puffy paint with no colour added, add glitter instead. Paint pictures on black paper

Children with visual impairment will particularly enjoy feeling their paintings when they are dry.

...and another thing

Try using this paint on small pieces of white cotton fabric. When dry, paint the fabric all over with diluted food colouring. When this is dry, wash the fabric. You should have some lovely batik patterns.

Early learning goals

PSED - continue to be interested, excited & motivated to learn
CLL - use talk to organise, sequence & clarify thinking, ideas, events;
 - write their own names & labels
K&U - investigate objects & materials by using all of their senses
 - select tools & techniques
Phys - use a range of equipment;
 - handle tools, objects, materials
Cr - explore colour, texture, shape, form & space
 - use their imagination in art
 - respond in a variety of ways to what they see, smell, touch & feel

Roll a Rag

Description

This method is a simple version of rag rolling. It is a technique which results in decorative paper with many uses.

What you need for simple rag rolling:

strips of fabric about 12" (30cm.) long. Tee shirt material works well
paper or plastic plates
paint in several colours
large sheets of thin paper
masking tape
feathers (optional)

aprons
table cover

Tips for success

Use thin fabric and mix the paint fairly thick. You might want to use a restricted range. Some options are:
 - red and two shades of green
 - white, silver and gold on black paper
 - dark and light blue and yellow

What you do

1. Tape a piece of paper down on the table.
2. Tie a knot in the middle of each piece of fabric.
3. Pour some paint on each plate.
4. Holding the ends of the fabric, dip the knot in the paint and roll it across the paper.
5. Re-dip and continue to roll.
6. Change colours and directions at will!
7. Work in lines, criss cross, waves.
8. Leave to dry and try repeating with another layer.

P.S. Try dipping a feather in paint and swirling it on the surface.

Use the paper to:
* wrap gifts
* back display boards and pictures
* make backings for calendars
* make table mats for parties
* redecorate your home corner

..and another thing

Other rolling techniques:
* marbles dipped in paint and rolled in a hoop or a bowl lined with paper
* tape paper on the floor or outside. Roll balls or bikes through paint and onto the paper.

Early learning goals

PSED - continue to be interested, excited & motivated to learn
CLL - use talk to organise, sequence & clarify thinking, ideas, events;
 - write their own names & labels
K&U - investigate objects & materials by using all of their senses
 - select tools & techniques
Phys - use a range of equipment;
 - handle tools, objects, materials
Cr - explore colour, texture, shape, form & space
 - use their imagination in art
 - respond in a variety of ways to what they see, smell, touch & feel

Glitter Pots

Description

Little pots for bulbs, table decorations or plants. Younger and older children will enjoy making this easy, good looking gift.

What you need for 25 glitter pots:

25 plastic plant pots, not too small or they are difficult to handle - 4" (10cm.) pots work well
all purpose filler or tile grout (from a DIY shop)
beads, buttons
sequins
glitter
old jewellery
shells and small polished stones
dry, dyed pasta shapes
small pieces of broken crockery or tiles (see below)
blunt knives or spreaders
a damp cloth
aprons, table cover

Tips for success

If you have chipped or broken items of crockery, break them into small pieces by putting in a strong plastic bag and hitting them with a hammer. (An adult activity!) Then check and remove any really sharp pieces before offering them to the children.

What you do

1. Cover the table.
2. Separate the sorts of mosaic pieces into dishes or empty plastic food trays.
3. Help each child to cover their pot with a thick layer of filler or grout, using a knife or spreader. Put the pot upside down to make it more stable.
4. Children can now press mosaic pieces into the the grout to make a pattern or design.
5. When they have finished, tidy up the filler if necessary and leave to dry.
6. When the pot is dry, wipe the mosaic with a damp cloth to remove any filler/grout film.
7. Coat the finished pot wit h dilute white glue or varnish to secure the pieces and give it a shine.

P.S. You can get old jewellery and bags of buttons from charity shops

PPS Dye dry pasta by shaking it in a plastic bag with a few drops of food colouring. Try little stars or alphabet letters.

...and another thing

Plant the pots with:
* early flowering bulbs
* house plant cuttings

or make a table decoration by putting a ball of clay or dough in the bottom and pushing in sprigs of foliage, holly, silver twigs etc.

Early learning goals

PSED - continue to be interested, excited & motivated to learn
CLL - extend their vocabulary, exploring the meanings of words
 - use talk to organise, sequence & clarify thinking, ideas, events;
Ma - use language to describe shape and size
K&U - investigate objects & materials by using all of their senses
Phys - use a range of equipment;
 - handle tools, objects, materials
Cr - explore colour, texture, shape, form & space
 - respond in a variety of ways to what they see, smell, touch & feel

Stand up Baby Snowmen

Description

Baby socks seldom have time to wear out before they are too small. Collect some and make these little snowmen to stand on a window sill.

What you need

enough white socks for one for each child
half as many coloured baby socks- each sock will make 2 hats
ribbon for a scarf
red or gold string
small buttons
dried beans, peas or rice
elastic bands
orange felt or pipe cleaners

scissors
glue and spreaders
fine markers

NB If you can't get enough baby socks, use towelling sports socks. You will need more filling and you will get 'grown up' snowmen.

Tips for success

Cut the bottom off a plastic cup to use as a funnel for filling the socks.
Don't put too much filling in, or the snowman will be too firm to stand properly.

What you do

1. Use your plastic cup funnel to help children fill the foot of the sock with peas, beans or rice.
2. Wind an elastic band round above the heel.
3. Trim off the top of the sock and check that the filling is right, and the snowman will stand up.
4. Tie ribbon tightly round the sock to separate the body from the head. This will make a scarf.
5. Cut a coloured sock at the heel to make two hats. Tie each piece at the top with red or gold string.
6. Place one hat on the snowman's head, rolling the edge like a bobble hat.
7. Stick some buttons on the snowman's front.
8. Draw a face, and make a nose from a small piece of felt or pipe cleaner to look like a carrot.
9. Stand the snowman on a shelf or window sill until it is time to take him or her home.

Children can do most of this activity with your help. Work in small groups (2 or 3 children at a time), so you have time to talk about what you are doing.

...and another thing

You could make a whole collection of these sock dolls.

Use red socks to make Santas, green to make elves, brown to make reindeer.

If you stuff the dolls with cotton wool, you can hang them on a tree.

Early learning goals

PSED - continue to be interested, excited & motivated to learn
CLL - use talk to organise, sequence & clarify thinking, ideas, events
Ma - use language to describe shape and size
K&U - investigate objects & materials by using all of their senses
 - select tools & techniques
Phys - use a range of equipment;
 - handle tools, objects, materials
Cr - explore colour, texture, shape, form & space
 - respond in a variety of ways to what they see, touch & feel

51

Storm in a Jam Jar!

Description

Two ways to make snowstorms for gifts or to keep.
The one without the glycerine is simpler for younger children.

What you need for Snowstorms:

small screw topped jars or baby food jars
water
glycerine (optional)
plaster of Paris or DIY filler
small twigs, holly or evergreen
a small cake decoration or plastic toy for each child
some dessicated coconut
sequins and glitter

a small bowl
an old spoon
a teaspoon
aprons, table cover

strong glue or a glue gun (adults only!) or waterproof tape to seal the lids

Tips for success

The water based storms are effective, but adding glycerine (available from chemists) makes the water thicker, so the 'snow' stays suspended for longer. It is quite safe to use!

What you do

1. Wash the jars and lids thoroughly. Children can help if supervised.
2. Make or buy a snowstorm so the children understand the process.
3. Mix some filler and spoon it into the bottom of the jar.
4. While it is still soft, push some twigs into the filler.
5. Push the plastic figure into the filler.
6. Leave over night to set.
7. Add water (or a mixture of half as much glycerine as water) to the jar.
8. Add coconut for 'snow', sequins, glitter etc.
9. Put the top back on and seal with waterproof tape or strong glue.
10. Decorate the lid with more sequins or paint mixed with white glue.

PS You can make these snowstorms upside down, by sticking the figure to the inside of the lid and filling the jar with water/water and glycerine. Add sequins etc. Screw the top onto the jar. Turn the jar upside down for the snow storm. <u>Make sure the lid is secure!</u>

...and another thing

You can make snowstorms without figures in them. Just fill the jars with the water and glycerine mixture and drop sparkly things in - sequins, star sequins, glitter, small shiny beads, 'pearls', or small decorations.

Decorate the tops with stickers or silver ric-rac tape or ribbon.

Early learning goals

<u>PSED</u> - continue to be interested, excited & motivated to learn
<u>CLL</u> - extend their vocabulary, exploring the meanings of words
<u>Ma</u> - use language to describe position
<u>K&U</u> - investigate objects & materials by using all of their senses
 - select tools & techniques
<u>Phys</u> - use a range of equipment;
 - handle tools, objects, materials
<u>Cr</u> - explore colour, texture, shape, form & space
 - respond in a variety of ways to what they see, hear, smell, touch & feel

Flying Santas

Description

These Santas really fly! Take them outside on a dry day and see how the streamers fly. Adult help is needed for this activity.

What you need for Flying Santas:

thin red card or heavy paper
white glue
felt pens
cotton wool
pink paint or sticky paper for faces
coloured wool or thread
stars or big sequins

plate to draw round (bigger plates make bigger Santas!)
saucer
scissors
stapler or sticky tape
pencil
aprons, table cover

Tips for success

You could use round sticky labels for the face and sticky stars for the ends of the streamers. This will enable children to do more of the activity without help.

What you do

1. For two Santa bodies, draw round the plate.
2. Cut out the circle and fold in half. Cut along the fold.
3. Stick or paint a pink circle in the middle of the straight edge of each for the face.
   Draw eyes and a smile.
4. Roll the card into a cone and stick or staple to fix.
5. Glue some cotton wool on for a beard.
6. Now draw round the saucer and cut it out for the wings.
7. Fold the circle in half and stick down.
8. Put a line of glue down the centre of this half circle, and stick the body to the wings.
9. Cut 6 lengths of wool, each about 20cm (8") long. Different colours look better.
10. Tie the ends together in a knot and stick the knot just inside the bottom of the body for a trail.
11. Stick sequins or stars to the end of each string. You could also put stars and sequins on his wings.
12. Push a small ball of plasticene into the top of the body, so he will fly straight.
13. Throw the Santa to make him fly.
    N.B. Treat this activity as disposable or don't suggest flying!

...and another thing

You can use this design for all sorts of cone figures - angels or tree fairies with doileys and glitter stuck on, wizards, spacemen etc. Or make snowmen in white card and read the Raymond Briggs story or watch the video.

Early learning goals

PSED - continue to be interested, excited & motivated to learn
CLL - interact with others, negotiating plans & activities
Ma - use language to describe the shape and size of shapes;
K&U - investigate objects & materials by using all of their senses
 - find out about, & identify some features of objects they observe;
 - build & construct with a wide range of objects, selecting appropriate resources
Phys - use a range of equipment;
 - handle construction

A Letter to Father Christmas

Description

Have fun <u>and</u> encourage writing letters by setting up a role play area and providing materials for writing letters to Father Christmas.

What you need for letter writing:

- a table or desk
- pens, pencils
- felt pens
- paper and envelopes (recycle these if money is tight)
- stamps (see below for ideas)
- address book
- selotape
- scissors
- photocopied lists of names (including Father Christmas)
- catalogues
- leaflets
- phone book and phone
- post box
- postal uniform and cap
- letter bag (a satchel is good)
- bike or van for deliveries

Tips for success

Make some stamps by 'sewing' across pieces of paper (sticky paper makes licky stamps). Without any cotton in the sewing machine, 'sew' lines of perforations across and down the paper. The children can then tear them off as they need them.

What you do

1. Talk with the children about what you need, and let them help you to collect the furniture and equipment.
2. Arrange a visit to a Post Office to see what happens there. You could collect some leaflets, take some photos, and they might give you some posters.
3. Go for a walk and look at a post box. Read and talk about the collection times. Watch for the post van or post delivery.
4. Discuss writing letters, and how the process works. Encourage children to 'have a go' at writing them selves, or making pictorial letters and lists.
5. Talk about and demonstrate how addresses work. Look at post codes and house numbers. Make a class address book, with everyone's address in it.
6. Look at catalogues and leaflets. Talk about different toys and games. Discuss favourites.
7. Talk about giving as well as getting. Make Christmas lists for other people as well as themselves.
8. Use the role play setting to make and deliver cards and letters to friends, staff and parents as well.

...and another thing

Make some stamps by using clip art from your computer to do a repeat of a head (a queen, king or famous person) or a snowman or other festive design. Perforate as described on the opposite page. Print in colour for a really good effect.

Early learning goals

PSED - work as part of a group/class
CLL - interact with others, negotiating plans & activities
- enjoy listening to and using spoken and written language, and turn to it in their play and learning
- use language to imagine & recreate roles & experiences
- attempt writing for various purposes
- write their own names & labels
K&U - find out about, & identify some features of events they see
Cr - use their imagination in imaginative & role play & stories

Story Time

Description

Convert your role play area into a festive setting for Christmas. Link it to a story or a pretend place and let your imagination run wild!

What you need for Story Time:

This list will enable you to make a Winter Wonderland with Santa Claus, his helpers and a North Pole setting. 'Father Christmas' by Raymond Briggs, and "A Letter to Father Christmas" by Rose Impey are good story starters.

white sheeting
cardboard cutout trees
silver and shiny drapes
silver stars on strings
artificial birds
lametta
window 'snow' spray
child size Santa suit (or red coat, hat and false beard)
suit for Mrs Santa
chair for Santa
bobble hats (with bells) for Santa's helpers
reindeer antlers on headbands
toys
boxes
wrapping paper, tape, string
clipboard and pens
labels for parcels
a truck for Santa's sleigh
reindeer food

Tips for success

This would give the setting for lots of stories. When you read a new story, put it in the role play area and check with the children that they have all the props they need to play out the new story.

What you do

1. Instead of a play screen, suspend white or shiny drapes from the ceiling, or over a clothes horse. Decorate the area with streamers, tinsel, spray snow. Hang stars, lametta and birds from strings, cover the floor with an old sheet for snow.
2. Get the children to help to arrange the furniture and props. They may suggest more props, and they will certainly have ideas about where to put things!
3. Read some stories about cold places
4. Talk about how Santa lives, looks after the reindeer, makes toys, what he eats, where he sleeps.
5. Talk about how animals and birds keep warm in winter.
6. Make some Bird Cake (recipe on page 62) and feed the birds.
7. Talk about the seasons, different clothes for cold weather.
8. Write letters to Father Christmas and have a post box.
9. Look at a globe and talk about the cold places and the hot places.
10. Practice wrapping presents, make labels and cards.
11. Link with outdoor play - have a post box and deliveries.

...and another thing

There are many Christmas stories suitable for role play settings. With older children, you might want to get involved in talking about fact and fiction, 'real' and 'pretend' places - without shattering any illusions of course!

Early learning goals

PSED - work as part of a group/class
CLL - interact with others, negotiating plans & activities
 - enjoy listening to and using spoken and written language, and turn to it in their play and learning
 - use language to imagine & recreate roles & experiences
 - attempt writing for various purposes
 - write their own names & labels
K&U - find out about, & identify some features of events they see
Cr - use their imagination in imaginative & role play & stories

Freezing Things

Description

If you have a cold snap, make these frozen decorations and hang them in the garden. They will glitter like glass, and the birds will love them!

What you need for frozen decorations:

plastic lids or shallow empty food trays
water
small sprigs of foliage, holly, ivy leaves etc
berries (rose hips, hawthorn berries)
shelled peanuts
raisins
wild bird food
string

scissors
plastic trays for sorting ingredients
aprons, table cover

Tips for success

If you choose trays with textured bases, they will make the ice look rippled or frosted. Always wash food containers thoroughly before re-using, and avoid those which have been used for meat.

What you do
1. Choose a lid and fill it with water.
2. Add seeds, berries, leaves etc.
3. Drape both ends of a piece of string in the lid, leaving the loop outside.
4. Freeze overnight.
5. In the morning, unmould the decorations and hang from trees, bushes and fences.
6. Watch them melt and then watch the birds come to eat up the nuts and berries.
7. Try putting food colouring in the water to make the decorations glow in jewel colours.

Make a frozen candle holder.
You need 2 plastic bowls, one bigger than the other.
1. Suspend the small bowl inside the bigger one with pieces of tape. Make sure the small bowl does not touch the sides or bottom of the big one.
2. Fill the space between the two bowls with tinsel, plastic Christmas decorations, beads and foliage.
3. Put in the freezer overnight. Then remove the bowls and put a night light or small candle inside.

Put this candle outside, or in a window (with a dish underneath!)

...and another thing
Birds welcome winter feeding, so try making bird cake (recipe on page 61). Make a bird feeder from a plastic bottle or a bird table hung from a branch or a hook. You could buy one of the feeders which stick onto the outside of the window, and watch the birds from inside.

Early learning goals
PSED - work as part of a group or class
 - understand that they and others have different needs, views, cultures & beliefs
CLL - extend their vocabulary, explore meanings & sounds of words
Ma - say and use number names in order in familiar contexts;
K&U - investigate objects & materials by using all of their senses
 - find out about, & identify some features of living things
Phys - use a range of equipment;
Cr - respond in a variety of ways to what they see, hear, touch & feel

Bird Cake

Description

Make a cake for the birds. This recipe is helpful in emphasising the effect of winter on your garden and the creatures who live there.

What you need for bird cake:

some of the following:
dried bird food
dried seed heads (grass, sweet corn, sunflower seeds etc)
peanuts (not salted)
bread crumbs
cake crumbs
coconut
chopped bacon rind
lard or white fat

a large bowl
a wooden spoon
a small bowl and a pan or bowl of very hot water (adult)
plastic pots or food containers
nets from fruit or vegetables
aprons, table cover

Tips for success

Melting fat can be done in a microwave or over a pan of hot water. Very young children should not be directly involved in this part of the recipe, but they can watch an adult if carefully supervised, and they enjoy seeing how the solid changes to liquid.

What you do

1. Put all the nuts and seeds and other ingredients in a big bowl and help the children to mix them thoroughly. Talk about the seeds and where they come from. Remind the children of spring and summer time when the flowers grow.
2. Melt the fat in a small bowl over hot water (adult only).
3. Add the melted fat to the seeds and other ingredients.
4. Mix well, so all the seeds etc are coated with fat. This will make the cake stick together.
5. Help the children to spoon the mixture into pots and other containers, pressing down well with the back of a spoon.
6. Put the pots in a cold place until the fat is set.
7. Tip the cake out onto the bird table, window sill or wall, and watch the birds come.

PS Don't forget that birds need water as well as food. This needs replacing every day.

Birds are only out of their winter nests and hiding places for a short time during winter days, so they need high calorie food to stay alive. They will also learn to rely on the food you put out, so remember to feed them regularly.

...and another thing

You can make this cake in a coconut. Make a hole in the coconut and drain the milk out. Then saw the coconut in half and fill each half with bird cake. Hang the coconuts up in the garden. You could also make strings of peanuts (in their shells) or popcorn.

Early learning goals

PSED - work as part of a group or class
CLL - interact with others, negotiating plans & activities & taking turns in conversations;
Ma - say and use number names in familiar contexts;
K&U - investigate objects & materials using all their senses
Phys - use a range of small and large equipment;
- handle tools, objects, & malleable materials safely & with increasing control.
Cr - use a widening range of materials, suitable tools, designing & making

More Christmas Activities

Description

You can give a Christmas flavour to many everyday number and language activities in your setting. Here are some ideas.

Counting Christmas

You need:
- some little zip Lock plastic bags
- small items for counting eg bells, pompoms, candles, little Christmas trees, tiny gift boxes, little decorations, cake decorations (snowmen, santas, sledges)

Put different numbers of identical items in each bag (eg 1 candle, 2 baubles, 3 snowmen, 4 bells, 5 trees)

Zip up the bags and use for counting and ordering.

You could add some number labels for older children.

Christmas feely bag

Make, buy or borrow a drawstring bag (big enough for several items). Collect some Christmas items - tinsel, a Santa hat, a small parcel, a stocking, a piece or greenery (not holly!), a little snowman, an unbreakable bauble, a candle, a walnut, a tangerine. Put in a few items at a time. Take turns to feel in the bag and name what you feel.

Repeating Christmas patterns

Cut some sponges or potatoes and do some repeating Christmas patterns. Stars, trees, stockings, baubles are all easy shapes to cut out. Print on paper, fabric, card or plastic. 'Read' the finished patterns to get the rhythm.

Scents of Christmas

Collect some little jars or pots. Put some Christmas smells inside and cover the top with a piece of fabric. Secure with an elastic bag. Guess the smell.
Try: orange flavouring, cinnamon, spices, perfumed Christmas oils, mincemeat.

Outside

Have an outside Christmas tree, hung with straw decorations and food for birds. Hang bells and plastic decorations from bushes and trees. Put up some outdoor Christmas lights.

Feed the birds

Thread seeds, peanuts, dried apple rings, coconut pieces and popcorn on strings. Hang from trees and bushes for the birds. Put out water as well.

Magic beans

Spray beans or pasta shapes with gold or silver paint and use them for counting and sorting.

Sparkle!

Add glitter, beads. sequins, star pasta to paint, dough and even sand. Let the children experience new textures.

More Sparkle!

Make hand and foot prints in silver and gold paint on black paper for a unique calendar picture. (Don't forget to add the date.)

Paper games

Use sheets of wrapping paper to make puzzles. Try this - buy 2 identical pieces of paper. Stick both on sheets of card. Cut one into a puzzle and use the other as a base board. Or mount identical small cards and use to play snap or pairs.

PS Use Christmas clip art to make labels, notices & letters to parents more festive.

Templates for rocking sheep card

NOTES

NOTES